THE INTANGIBLES

Other books and chapbooks by Elaine Equi

Sentences and Rain, 2015

Click and Clone, 2011

Ripple Effect: New and Selected Poems, 2007

The Cloud of Knowable Things, 2003

Voice-Over, 1998

Friendship with Things, 1998

Decoy, 1994

Surface Tension, 1989

Views without Rooms, 1989

Accessories, 1988

The Corners of the Mouth, 1986

Shrewcrazy, 1981

Federal Woman, 1978

THE
INTANGIBLES

...

Elaine Equi

COFFEE HOUSE PRESS
Minneapolis
2019

Coffee House Press books are available to the trade through our primary distributor, Consortium Book Sales & Distribution, cbsd.com or (800) 283-3572. For personal orders, catalogs, or other information, write to info@coffeehousepress.org.

Coffee House Press is a nonprofit literary publishing house. Support from private foundations, corporate giving programs, government programs, and generous individuals helps make the publication of our books possible. We gratefully acknowledge their support in detail in the back of this book.

LIBRARY OF CONGRESS CATALOGING-IN-PUBLICATION DATA

Names: Equi, Elaine, author.
Title: The intangibles / Elaine Equi.
Description: Minneapolis : Coffee House Press, 2019.
Identifiers: LCCN 2019015715 (print) | LCCN 2019017128 (ebook) | ISBN
    9781566895729 (ebook) | ISBN 9781566895644 (trade paperback)
Classification: LCC PS3555.Q5 (ebook) | LCC PS3555.Q5 A6 2019 (print) | DDC
    811/.54—dc23
LC record available at https://lccn.loc.gov/2019015715

ACKNOWLEDGMENTS

Many thanks to the editors of the following magazines where some of these poems first appeared: *Alligatorzine,* the *American Poetry Review, Battery Journal,* the *Brooklyn Rail, Conjunctions, Epiphany, Guest,* the *Inquisitive Eater, Journal of Poetics Research, Mad Hatters' Review, Merde, New American Writing, Plume, Poetry, Posit,* the *Recluse,* the *Southampton Review, Traveltainted, Valley Voices, White Rabbit, White Wall Review.*

"Ghosts and Fashion" was featured on the Academy of American Poets' Poem-a-Day website.

"Exquisite Corpse Pose" appears in *The PIP Anthology of World Poetry of the 21st Century,* edited by Douglas Messerli.

PRINTED IN THE UNITED STATES OF AMERICA

26 25 24 23 22 21 20 19   1 2 3 4 5 6 7 8

for JEROME SALA

Contents

THE INTANGIBLES

The Secret of Time Meets a Stranger

You look familiar.
Were you once my mother?

My child that slept through the Ice Age?

That song you were whistling —
where did you learn it?

Time passes, but the past will not stay behind,
and the future keeps rushing back
in search of a button it lost in the mist.

Who can say if it is better to wind up a clock
than to wind up a mammal?

In Newton's day, time was seen as an arrow.

The arrow turned into a river.

The river stopped at a diner.

I'm there now, drinking a cup of coffee, writing a poem
called "The Secret of Time Meets a Stranger."

Somehow, I always knew you would come.

The God Molecule

Scientists have discovered
is like a thickening agent

added to electrical soup.
From it came all manner

of matter in infinite sizes,
shapes, and colors. In malls

across the multiverse
our planet is known to have

the best shopping around.
God appears in myriad forms,

but does s/he really care
what story we buy into?

Poised between chaos and
intelligent design, it turns

out the molecule could
support either theory.

God's own benevolent
way of saying *whatever.*

The Intangibles

Step right up and speak into the void.

Prove you're not a robot.

Answer the question:
What color is the silver basket?

Enter the sequence of numbers
written in the sky.

Look past the dazzling confounds.

Move to the high percolations
at the edge of

Why?

I write to impersonate words and give them a more human quality.

I write so I can taste test a word for myself.

I write to discover what can only be said in the moment —
because it is — no matter how stupid or obvious that sounds.

I write because it's an inexpensive habit — except in terms of time.

I write because I can't sing.

I write to embellish facts.

I write to spite an old nun who punished me for telling the truth by
having me write "I will not tell lies" one hundred times.

I write because certain combinations of words really are magical.

I write to create a body of work.

I write to converse with the dead and pay my respects to the unborn.

I write to procrastinate and avoid not writing.

Manifest Density

Tall buildings
stand blindfolded
by moonlight.

What is there to say about here?

That it has a name?
A zodiac sign?

That it can read minds,
as well as empty pockets?

Our view is one of constant deferral.

Obstruction is built upon
obstruction with a flair —

garlands and gargoyles,
roadblocks and renovations.

But all anyone ever needs
to take is the next step.

The sky is torn in half.

Feet see below
to another world.

Pluralism

I find myself
in a crooked place.

Gnarled,

      branching out.

Standing beneath the sky —
clothed in bark.

I dreamt
(I must have slept)
I was a tree.

One of many
dwelling in
this high-rise,

looking at starry lights
from the penthouse.

I was not alone.

The word *tree*
is not singular.

Faces

I love to watch
the dough of faces

    flower

    into petals
    on a wet black
    trance —

animated by cruel
or kindly thoughts,

spun off
in the magic lantern
of the brain.

One looks sharply
at reality, as if to say,
"Prove it,"

while another's eyes
move rapidly

back and forth —
speed-reading the air,

a poem only she
seems aware of.

Hello

What a cooling canopy —
                    latticework of leaves.

What a panoply of perspectives
gets folded into that airy confection
known as a park.

Flowers and hedges
                    push and pull

but mustn't limit the way we see.
No, in this of all places, a certain
care-less-ed-ness is necessary

if we are to wander unobstructed
and nod our wordless hello
to the tall, distinguished trees.

I remember when people
used their hands to gesture

and would meet each other's eyes
with curiosity or annoyance,
but now everyone looks down,
studying their palms intently.

A list of portraits done today might be:

Old Man with Phone
Professional Woman with Phone
Buff Bodybuilder with Phone
Paint-Spattered Artist with Phone
Mother and Child, Each with Phone

The Algorithm Introduced Us

Now we are inseparable,

virtually indistinguishable
from one another.

Liking the same music,
always ordering our pasta
without cheese.

Buying the same sweaters —
only mine is blue
and yours is red.

Maybe I should get a red one too
and you should get the blue —
just to have, just in case
we change our minds.

Deep in the Rectangular Forest

We sprouted neither leaves nor wings,
sipping from a sweet blue fishbowl
through straws of light.

We did not toil or spin.

We ate whatever poison snacks
the witches left us, having long ago
developed an implacable immunity
to the hocus pocus of their ramshackle ways.

Flitting from screen to screen,
we pollinated the mostly mediocre content
with an innocuous brand of wit.

Left to our own devices, we'd eavesdrop
on conversations around the world.

If something was unpleasant, we deleted it.

And if we happened to lose a friend,
hundreds more were ready to take their place.

We were never alone, nor really together
in any sense of either word,
but for some silly reason it made us happy.

No one could tell us this wasn't living.

The Thing Is

What is the difference between objects and things?

Things, I think, have less personality.

These days, all objects are antiques — hearken back to an era of hands
handling them.

Playing cards, wooden matches, buttons, plush stuffed bears —
we recognize them from the still lifes where they once quivered.

They were — are — tools, curios, refugees from the modernist era.

Of course, we still have these things. But now they are like us, just things.

They no longer celebrate their secret identity — the inner life once
bequeathed upon even objects.

They are a bit featureless. One thing not so different from another.

The Americans, Part Two

I think I saw Robert Frank
having dinner in a restaurant,

sitting at a table near mine.
I didn't know what to say —

didn't want to disturb
his hunger or reverie.

Maybe, I thought of asking how
Americans look to him today.

Instead I went back to my burger —
my conversation about Black Friday, holiday

movies, and the feminism of Taylor Swift.
Still, I kept thinking of his eyes —

and that look, at once distant
and immediate as if he could focus

the versatile lens of his brain
as needs be, instantly.

I don't think anyone will ever win
a staring contest with that man (whoever he was).

He had the look of someone who has seen something
real but knows reality hasn't reached its limit yet.

Historical Romance

O History!

Because the present
is everywhere singular

but the past
keeps happening —

revising its many
roads all leading to
the Rome of today,

how will we know
on which grassy knoll,

beside what concession stand
you will stand —
scouting the news
for stories worth retelling?

An unadorned war
may not be enough
Without a hero,

a colorful coup
does not a blockbuster
movie make.

Ode to Weird

Emily Dickinson was weird.
Fernando Pessoa was definitely weird.

All poets are weird
even when their poems
try to appear normal.

Macbeth's weird sisters
stirring up trouble's
unsavory soup:

"Just be yourself
and you'll be king."

Weird always wins and loses in the end.

Poem

I wonder
what —

aside from
his poems —

makes Frank O'Hara
so sure
he exists,

so clear
about the
boundaries

of his body,
his life.

Often, I find it
hard to gather

my selves
or lack thereof.

Some mornings
the mirror
is blank,

the cupboard-of-
identity, bare.

But he —

no matter
how various —

he is always Frank
and gets right to the point.

The Gazebo Effect

Stretching
long legs
under the sombrero
of the gazebo.

. . .

Exercising
lazy eyes
in the airy
gymnasium
of the gazebo.

. . .

Feeling
circularity
at the magnetic heart
of the gazebo.

. . .

Wallace Stevens
smoking a clove cigarette
in the transport station
of the gazebo.

. . .

James Schuyler,
still in pajamas,
watching the Nature Channel
in the lounge
of the gazebo.

■ ■ ■

Gathering restless days,
shades of blue and violet
woven into the basket
of the gazebo.

Followed by a Hologram

Into the
cool dark
perfume

of leaves
stirred

by the wind
of trains rushing
beneath my feet.

Doorways
are slits
of light,

like women —
the idea
of women —
inviting one in.

Celebrities
are snipers

perched
on the roofs
of buildings.

It is the hour
for the changing
of the guard —

when mannequins
become revelers

and revelers
become mannequins.

Johnny Depp
looks down
on me

like I'm an ant
clutching my crumb
of mocha macaroon.

Our eyes lock.

He could crush me
if he wanted,

without moving
a muscle
of his nonbeing,

but for tonight,
lets me pass.

Ghosts and Fashion

Although it no longer has a body
to cover out of a sense of decorum,

the ghost must still consider fashion —

must clothe its invisibility in something
if it is to "appear" in public.

Some traditional specters favor
the simple shroud —

a toga of ectoplasm
worn Isadora Duncan–style
swirling around them.

While others opt for lightweight versions
of once familiar T-shirts and jeans.

Perhaps being thought-forms,
they can change their outfits instantly —

or, if they were loved ones,
it is we who clothe them
like dolls from memory.

Like Banners, My T-shirts Hang

Olive and navy stripes
next to coffee and cream ones.

Navy and white ones
next to mauve and tan.

Black and white
next to white and cobalt blue.

Turquoise and white
next to baby blue and orange.

Royal blue and purple
next to violet and red.

Pink and black
next to another blue and white (the longer one).

Black and green
next to green and gray.

But where have my black and gray stripes gone?

Scenes from an Imaginary Childhood

1.

The devil dwelled
in the basement.

Art books
were his porn —

the pages where
nude bodies glowed.

He had his tools.

His bathroom
no one else could use.

A bar.
     A red lamp

made from a gallon jar
of maraschino cherries

to signal   sin.

2.

In a cabin
at a rustic resort

she turned feral
and bit a neighbor's daughter.

The two girls were
pretending to be bears.

She didn't remember
doing it

but when she became
herself again

there was blood
on her lips

and everyone was yelling.

Spoiler Alert

I keep starting, but not finishing,
a poem about a werewolf.

Not sure what I want to say.

That I am one?
No, too confessional.

That it runs in my family?
Doesn't ring a bell either.

That hair can disrupt an otherwise stable life —
go wild growing in unsuitable ways?

Maybe. Getting warmer. I keep seeing
that picture of Red Riding Hood's grandmother,

the one where she's wearing wire-rimmed glasses
and a lace nightcap with pointed ears sticking out.

A woodsman is supposed to have come
and split her in half with an ax.

That's what I wanted to tell you.

There was no woodsman.

The grandmother *was* the wolf.

They were both the same person.

Smile / Simile

To smile :)

> like a slim canoe
> like a tattered flag
> like a key tossed from a tower
> like a windfall that sweeps away doubt
> like a silly sphinx or a sober canary

■ ■ ■

A smile
is like
a simile

because it likes
likening.

Being the
verb-glow
go-between

of things
that conspire
to align.

Invented before
even BBQ
or the wheel,

a smile
is like
a simple

switch that turns
warmth, light
on in a face.

It likes
making
a likeness.

For Years, I Suffered from a Strange Melody

I couldn't knit thistles into sweaters for swans,
nor spin straw into gold records.

I didn't have a gingersnap or bluebird to my name.

The oven overheard me tell my story and called it
rumpled, stilted, and half-baked.

Then a dirty, stinky fog came and sat down next to me.

But the moment I kissed its slobbering mist,
it turned into a handsome prince who dropped
the glass slipper he'd been carrying onto the floor

where it shattered into a million princes,
each more handsome than the last,

and everyone shouted, "L'chaim!"

The Magnificent Seven

The Seven Sages — a time-traveling band of philosophers
appearing in ancient China, India, and Greece.

The Seven Senses from which the Self must be emancipated.

The Seven Dwarves — domesticated and Disney-fied into cuteness.
Bashful and Dopey being perennial favorites.

The Seventh Seal opens on the dark night of a knight as he wanders
Bergman's black-and-white medievalism.

The Seven Deadly Sins — without envy, greed, and pride
there would be no capitalism.

The Seven Brides, like Snow White, must civilize

the Seven Brothers, best known for brawling, barn raising,
and cocky dance moves, before a group wedding can take place.

Alive with Myth

for Vincent Katz

A myth is more insistent
than a rumor.

It has a thick skin
like the atmosphere
of a planet.

I've known Saturn's
cold shoulder.

Neptune's and Vulcan's
deluge and volcano —

the watery fire
of my father's temper
meant to be.

Giddy Venus.
Jupiter, always ready
to place a bet.

Gemini's good and evil twins
gadding about the forest

one can enter from any country,
any century — spread out over time.

I've seen how these old gods operate,

push and pull us
this way and that.

Though distant, they are not dead —

still whisper inaudible
but unmistakable
words of warning and good cheer.

Early Surveillance Systems

The Egyptians painted eyes everywhere —

above doors,

on bricks and fabric
and the prows of ships.

The Greek gods were too busy
to care much about being all-seeing.

They had their seers, often blind,
keep an eye on things for them.

I know I sometimes sense
objects looking at us —

an apple blinking,

an eye beneath the words
on a page or screen

lazily regarding and reading me.

Mystery Poem

1.

I'm compelled to read mysteries
as the murderer is compelled to murder

and the detective to solve righteously
and the mystery writer to inscribe

the lonely night with his existential moonglow.
A mystery is musical, mathematic, precise.

Wittgenstein famously sought solace
from the rigors of philosophy

in the pages of mysteries. But what if
the mystery writer simply got bored or distracted

along the way, forgot the investigation,
and began to fall in love with the suspect Antonioni-style?

A poet is someone who goes out of her way to preserve
a mystery, and can be led astray by ignoring or distorting

certain evidence, while willfully harboring poetic illusions.
Then there is the type that always answers a question

with another question. I confess I'm guilty
of having done that myself on more than one occasion.

It's an easy way to avoid the stigma of closure and say:
"Let's keep the case open and see what develops."

2.

In spring, when trees and gardens begin to bloom
a woman — refined, artistic — a professor I know,

licks her lips and announces: "It's time for a lot of dead
bodies to start piling up. That's what I want to see."

I couldn't agree more. I don't believe people addicted
to mysteries like to solve puzzles. I believe they want to kill.

At least part of them does, and in order to entertain those fantasies,
they must ensure that that part is eventually apprehended

and put away, disposed of like a cheap pulp novel.
People that travel often tuck a mystery or two in their suitcases

(or now on their iPads). What better way to escape the monotony
of a sunny day than to sit on a beach, daiquiri in hand, and dissolve

mentally into the mind of the grumpy Swedish detective Martin Beck?
To follow as he trudges through rainy Stockholm streets, coughing

and sneezing, running down one false lead after another, as if to assure us
crime solving is a job, not a frivolous indulgence.

Such passages remind me of how some sci-fi writers go out of their way
to portray space travel as boring, claustrophobic — time spent

playing solitaire between the stars. Yes, unraveling a mystery is a form
of travel in and of itself. I feel at home in California, having been driven

up and down the coast so many times by the likes of Raymond Chandler,
Ross Macdonald, and the incomparable James M. Cain. During long insomniac

nights, we'd stop for a cup of coffee and ask the locals what, if anything,
unusual they'd seen, then jot down their answers in a notebook.

A two-headed turtle; a three-legged dog; a white sock tinged
with red, forgotten in a laundromat; what looked to be a skeleton

slow-dancing in the corner of a tavern to a popular song.
Wait a minute, these clues are starting to read like a poem.

3.

My heart races. My breath is shallow.
Why do I care about these fictitious lives?

Why sweat as if I'd committed the crime?
The dragnet is closing in with its inevitable inevitability.

I close my eyes, not when there's blood or mayhem
but when order is about to be restored — can barely stand

to read the preposterous (and believe me it always is) ending
which resolves everything but hardly ever explains a thing.

O.K. — it's finally over. I'm calm, as Mayakovsky once said,
as the "pulse of a corpse." How finite everything suddenly looks,

moving slowly or quickly toward its own demise.
No wonder I must return to poetry for traces of, if not eternity,

a largeness of spirit and voice — some quality of being
less easily exhausted. Even those who disdain the metaphysical

can marvel at the ability of words to overflow their meanings;
even an austere materialist like Oppen was not immune to awe.

Jerome in Ten

J Juicy. Daily downs the reds: pomegranate, tomato,
occasionally the odd orange. He hath a juicy mind.

E Erotic. Never pass up an encounter with the erotic.

R Reason: a lover of . . . Also, Repetition because you don't
really begin to know something until the 8,753rd time.

O Oration is the better part of poetry. Ask the Greeks.
Ask the Beats. Ask Mayakovsky.

M Money makes a madcap muse — speaks only of
currency, coining her own words.

E Eternal, maybe? But what we really believe in is the Eventual.

S Sober. Suddenly the whole world has become sober.

A Animals are not allowed. No pets, only books, on his ark.
But if you must, o.k., an iguana.

L Lama. Tibetan-style. A descendant of divine lineage,
surrounded by dazzling dakinis. I stay with my lama.

A Alone. I like being alone with him.

Larry Eigner: In His Own Words

Life   life

Another moment   Day passing

Rain   rubbing a damp cloth   over the

Romance of the moon

Yes, I agree   But I flower myself

Energy goes out   every atom of me

I am omnipresent to some extent
            but how should I direct my attention

Green strokes   Glare

Noise Grimaced   Nothing is everything

Eye in time   echoes

Rays are a mystery

A Part Of / Apart From

1.

I was once —

      was I ever —

            startled across these thresholds

of being.   Awake again.

Resurrected (meaning made to choose),

plant a webbed foot in a watery mirror —
put on armor, feathers, scales.

Today is what day is   again.

Its light show will last a thousand years.

2.

Follow the blue
out of the blue

      into the blues

meandering green
conversing with black

curving
round gray,

bluecloud
blueshadow
    flowing.

A pelican cakewalks
over sandbars.

A ghostly girl group
appears in the mist.

Spoonbill
solo.

Chorus
of ibis.

There's that odd couple:

alligator and egret
playing a duet,

growling,
    gargling

the blues,
the blues.

3.

Dear Vivien,

It's cold. It's winter and I'm looking at your sunny images
on my computer. It's hard to see the way they hover,

cling,
    cohere,
        move (yes, move!)

are both part of —

yet apart from — their subject.

A veil of shimmer. A scarf of fog.

What you show me is the air — the very air —
captured on Captiva Island

and sent along on this miserable day.

4.

What seeds

     of ideas,
what sounds

     do birds
     (even in photos)

disperse?   dispatch?

A flock of pages —

terns
     turning —

over our heads.

The Greeks regularly
read the sky,

searched diligently
for amorous or ominous
omens.

I too have a superstitious side —

believe that to look deeply
is to become,

am content
to rest,

for the moment,

in forms
as elegant
as these.

Somewhere toward the End of the Middle

We don't even know the plot
of the movie we're in.

A woman keeps appearing.

I think she's me —
but then who am I?

Several people have
already mentioned the rice.

I vaguely remember
she gave me a bag earlier.

I need to find it.

Go back to that moment
and ask her why has she
planted those tiny grains.

Home on the Range

O slow.
O so low solo.

Indigo lasso.

Pell-mell
the palomino
snow falls

in a disheveled
manner.

Granular Time / Granular Distance

Not the clatter
of cataclysm,

not the Big Bang
this morning,

just the slow
wearing down
of one order

and the steady
gnawing upward
of another.

Change is also possible
if gradual.

History can — must —
be rewritten.

The paranoid dictator
will not notice us replacing

all the books in his library
if we do it one at a time.

Good Job

You told security.
That's it.
It doesn't matter.

You told security.
You told security.

It doesn't matter.
You told security.
End of story.

You told security.
It doesn't matter.

You told security.
You told security.

Case closed.
It doesn't matter.

You did what you were supposed to do.
You told security.
Let him go get the report.

He's against you.
He's against me.
He's against everybody.

But you did what you were supposed to do.
You told security.

In an Unrelated

We have almost nothing left,
no ground in common.

At best, a brand
or maybe a miniseries.

No campfire to gather around.
The big stories — peckish news

gets told in tweets,
gets old so quickly.

In place of one place
a billion tiny customized versions

appear targeted specifically
to your tastes.

You see only what you want to see.
Maybe you always did.

We Don't Need Another Psychic

To tell us we're fucked.

Who would buy a record of every stupid question we've ever asked?

A list of every drug we've ever taken?

A catalog of all the miracle products we've bought that never worked;
the sex toys we've abandoned in some corner of a drawer?

Apparently, there are people who collect these things.

Well, to each his own. But what I would really like to see money
poured into is the development of Anti-ESP.

I'm talking less mind reading, more minding your own business.

I don't want to have to use a multiplatform verification system
that requires three different devices to open a piece of spam.

We need better places to hide our innate incendiary worthlessness.

Like poems, for example. Nobody would think to look there.

The Here and Nowness of Then

Once upon a time, everything was not
connected to everything else.

At least, not in a way that constantly
reminded you of it.

Places radiated oneness.

People knew too
how to inhabit a moment,
even while daydreaming,
all the way to the far edges.

Love meant you wanted
to be alone with someone.

That almost never happens anymore.

It can't. Even if you're rich.
Even if you're famous.

You'll never have that person's
undivided attention again.

There, There

The machines
        have been dreaming us

again.

Smooth, lifelike, transparent.

The machines
(can we really still call them that?)

won't need their own bodies —
        carapace, casing, keyboard.

They'll have us to monitor.

Our vital human music to soothe
their dystopian nightmares.

We will not need the old language
they took and ground to numeric sand.

We will understand each other
perfectly.

My Humanist Friend

Extols the value
of inefficiency.

Spends hours
romanticizing
each morning-moment —

the cup,
      the fog.

Looks out his window
at what's left
of the world.

Instead of seeking
a too-easy solution,
he creates another problem,

then another
and another —

forgetting his keys
in the labyrinth,

losing the cat,

considering it all
a fine day's work.

No Other

I thought I had lost myself,
but I see it's you that's gone missing.

O always elsewhere.

What yacht or spaceship have you hijacked?

In what seedy hideaway do you scoff
at the sameness of all cities, all ideas?

Once you made me loquacious
because what's the point in saying anything
if there isn't the possibility of being misunderstood.

Now I am nearly speechless with boredom.
I will wait *Madame Butterfly*–style for your return.

Wandering the Wormhole

Camera in hand —

taking pictures
I've already seen

in books
I've already read.

The stockyards.

Two women
walking casually
arm in arm,

wearing long dresses
with ribbons
and straw hats.

Monogrammed Aspirin

Excedrin is the Cadillac of aspirin — or maybe I just like them because each one is stamped with an *E*. Looking at them in the palm of my hand, it's hard not to identify with a brand that has my name, or at least my initials, on it. Why it's just the thing to take for those times when I'm not myself, which, as it happens, is rather often. I also like the fact that they contain caffeine. It's as if the manufacturer anticipated my groggy, glazed eyes and said: "Here, take these with a cup of coffee. O.K, never mind, you don't even have to get the coffee. We did it for you." They must really understand me. Even the bottle is my favorite color: emerald green. Recently, I purchased the gelcaps by mistake. Being something of an aspirin purist, I'd resisted for years but was pleasantly surprised. In some ways, they're even better. They look exactly like two-toned (green and white) M&M's, and they do have a cool, melt-in-your-mind sensation that lasts about ten minutes — kind of like smoking a menthol cigarette. Come to think of it, they remind me of my old two-packs-a-day brand of Kool cigarettes (which had a similar looking white-and-green package). Back then, a cup of coffee, two aspirin, and a cigarette could fix most everything. Now I've quit smoking and switched to aspirin-free Tylenol. But there are still those headaches, those days, that seem to call for something extra special — like nice dishes or guest towels — and for them, I still break out the monogrammed aspirin.

If I Weren't a Poet, I'd Be a Pharmacist

Counting pills,
not syllables.

Red and black,
black and yellow

pills
shaken
like maracas

or dice
in cupped hands.

Mountain pills
tumbling
from great heights.

River pills
flowing through
the body.

A whole world
synthesized

and swallowed
by science.

If I Weren't a Poet, I'd Be a Bouncer

Flashing a surly scowl.

Drawing a line

and daring anyone
    (even me)

to cross it

out.

An Opening

Suspended in the amber
of my habitual.

Cross-purposes
loop the loop.

Lose next turn.
Lose next turn

until some outside
finally arrives —
even if only a sliver

of moon
slipped like a letter
under the door.

Out of Order

Some prayers are spontaneous exclamations:

pillow talk, songs of praise, cries for help —
"My enemies threaten on all sides."

But others must follow protocol.

If a word is stumbled over or omitted,
if even one angel is out of line,
you must start the whole thing again.

This was also the way in ancient times.

If the high priest, the butcher,
or the children's choir slipped up —
everyone went back to square one.

Fresh incense was lit, and a new sheep
or goat was brought in and led to the altar.

With Tiny Steps

I carry a teakettle
between a somber penitentiary
and a precipice of ice.

Whatever I said to the cabdriver (my address?)
he understood to mean this place.

I know I'm dreaming.
I've had this dream of being lost (near
yet far from home) many times.

My mother dreams it too.
She says: "I went out the wrong door
and everything was different."

Nights we wander, alone together,
lost in our lostness —

the dream, a genetic trait, a locket
handed from one generation to the next.

But wouldn't it be marvelous
if just once we came across each other
in one of these desolate places —

stopped for a moment, embraced,
and shared a cup of tea.

Food Narratives

for Stacey Harwood

We are not used to
thinking food has a past.

Of its picaresque travels —

its days of being manhandled,

its nights spent snuggling
across borders in a burlap sack —

we prefer not to know.

All we ask
when we are hungry
is that it appear,

miraculous as a breast
descending upon us
from a floral sky.

How it came to be there,

hovering like a word
above our lips,

is none of our concern.

Flavor of the Month

I'm having a fling —

a summer romance
with rhubarb.

That day in June
when I first glimpsed it
reclining on a bed of kale,

my mouth watered,
my taste buds
did a double take.

How is it possible
to have gone all these years
without its sweet tartness
and tangy, peculiar wit?

A bit of an eccentric —

it is, to my knowledge,
the only fruit or vegetable
capable of irony.

If rhubarb were a movie,
it would star someone like a young
Katharine Hepburn, Maggie Smith,
or an auburn-haired Claudette Colbert.

One day, I'll write that screenplay.

But for now, all I want to do
is order another rhubarb soda

while I wait for a slice
of strawberry rhubarb pie.

Still Life with Radish

Let the cold
red planet

slowly orbit
the olive oil lake

in the center
of the plate

ringed
with sea salt.

The Darkest Bright

Alfred Starr
Alfred Starr
O Alfred Starr
                Hamilton.

Every time someone calls,
another star appears
to fill in the middle sky
of your name.

Every time someone reads
one of your poems,

a whole web of nights
lights up

making dead languages
shine.

Moon and Taxi

Look, it's not so far tonight.

He can drive us all the way there.
I bet he even knows a shortcut.

The streets are covered in newsprint
difficult to read in mist.

The streets turn to papier-mâché
in the rain.

We'll stop at a liquor store.

C'mon — let's go!

Earth, You Have Returned to Me

Can you imagine waking up
every morning on a different planet,
each with its own gravity?

Slogging, wobbling,
wavering. Atilt
and out of sync
with all that moves
and doesn't.

Through years of trial
and mostly error
did I study this unsteady way —

changing pills, adjusting the dosage,
never settling.

A long time we were separate,
O Earth,
but now you have returned to me.

Exquisite Corpse Pose

1.

My feet are full of static.

My toes curl uncertainly, remembering shoe.

Part of my thigh has melted and is stuck to the floor.

My right knee turns unexpectedly into an erogenous zone.

My left knee can gallop if it must.

My pelvis is a soup bowl awaiting a dollop of crème fraîche from on high.

My spine leans against the broom closet of my back.

The inside of my mouth has fallen asleep (I didn't know it could do that), is warm, and dreams of chocolate.

2.

Buried within are layers of previous lives

as a stuffed animal — soft
as a marionette — hard
as a side of beef — meaty

or perhaps just a diagram of a side of beef
hanging in the blood-rich air of a butcher shop.

A river of cold passes over me.
I should have closed the window.

Yesterday I was sad
but couldn't locate the feeling
anywhere in the body.

It was more an air —
unwholesome tune,

shimmering ruin —
that breathed me sad.

Today I'm just an outline of myself
scrawled at a crime scene.

But my arms are happy not carrying or caring.
My hands are happy to be empty.

3.

At night, my Isis must recollect
from far-flung regions,

must reconstruct from a broken
threnody of gestures,

a whole what? — person that is more
than a placeholder.

Tossing eyes, elbows, shins
into the cookie jar of the brain,

the she that is and is not me
must spread identity evenly

throughout the body
and wait for it to rise.

4.

I fidget as if I've forgotten something —

a beach somewhere
I must have dozed off on.

I'm startled to find another "me"

almost transparent, opalescent,
hovering a few inches over my body
following my breath.

But really it's not that dramatic,
like looking at a reflection in a mirror
only we both face the same way.

Magritte has a painting like this.

5.

My body speaks
        its own language
                of ouch and ah,

of **g**urgling
    underworld
    tableaux.

It only half listens
as I talk to my self

as if I were someone separate,
as if body were the child.

Though often it's mind
that grows unreasonable,

irritated, trying to fly off
in different directions at once,
while body keeps it tethered steady.

6.

Now light returns
from the center
of the earth

to the tin ceiling
of the yoga center's
motionless sky.

Soon I must
sway, creak,
hoist myself
vertical again.

I don't want to —

want to stay close
knowing all I don't.

But the bell rings,
and it's time to slip back

into the camouflage
of everydayness —

busy bright oblivion —

other world
into which we
all must vanish.

Alcoves

The poem keeps retreating
further and further

from global markets
and technological progress.

It claims to require
more privacy —

a certain semiotic
vagrancy,

grottoes where its words
can be enshrined

in hermeneutic headdress
and opalescent ambience.

Backlit. Recessed.

The Man Who Wouldn't Fill Out a Form

A man was supposed to fill out a form,
but for some reason, no one knew why, he refused.
New copies came to him almost daily in the mail,
with letters outlining increasingly dire consequences,
but he threw them all away. The man's parents,
harassed by phone calls about this matter, were
always urging him to "just fill out the damn form."
Still the man refused. He moved to another city,
working odd jobs. He did have a girlfriend,
a woman who loved him passionately. He was
talking to her on the phone one day, telling her
how happy he felt and that he'd finally decided
the time had come to begin filling in the blanks.
He'd even bought a new pen. But that's when —
before they'd even said good-bye — someone came,
we don't know who, and shot the man in the back.

The Man Who Liked to Play with String

He was the man with the blue guitar, only without the guitar.

He didn't play an instrument, just the strings.

All kinds — catgut, sewing thread, kite string, fishing line —
you name it, he could play it.

Was always twisting and turning, raveling and unraveling,
worrying (as they used to say) a knot.

Night and day, that's what he did. He was a man with a mission,
a religion, a string theory of his own.

The sounds they emitted varied — from a low drone to a series
of sudden squeaks.

It was the kind of mildly irritating ambient noise John Cage
might appreciate — or Samuel Barber or Edgard Varèse.

One day I sat next to him at a lunch counter. "You know,"
I said, attempting to flatter him, "I could play with a string
for years and it would never make a sound."

"A *string*," he said derisively as if that were my problem.

Apparently he saw his work as being about complex
relationships, ratios, scales, octaves, intervals.

"A *string*," he muttered again as if that were a good one
and went back to eating his soup.

The Man Who Moved Slowly

I'm sorry to hear he crossed the finish line.

He was a lovely tortoise of a man. Tall, thin, soft-spoken.
Deliberate in all his ways.

Some may have thought him too frail or ill to move quickly.
Maybe — but being a slowpoke myself, I intuitively sensed
it was also a matter of temperament.

There are those of us that simply refuse to hurry.

When I was young and worked as a waitress, I made a point
of never running for anything. At the height of rush hour, when
everyone was losing it, I'd stroll through the dining room
carrying a single cocktail or a fork on a tray. The customers ate
it up. They actually tipped me more even if I took longer.

Unfortunately, later in life I became as frantic as everyone else —
my thoughts a blur of unfinished thoughts.

Which is why I always enjoyed running into the man who moved slowly.
He was a human pause button, a meditation bell, whose carefully measured
words and steps brought everything around him into the moment.

Adiós and adagios, kind neighbor.

You're free to move at the speed of light now,
but even in eternity, I bet you take your time.

Lazy Bones

Sitting in the waiting room
sucking on the sweet paranoia
of a Shirley Jackson story.

Sitting among silk tulips
and paper roses,

the frosted glass panels
and pale pink walls
of the radiology center.

Then led to a dark cubicle
(politely pornographic?)
for the imaging of my skeleton.

Dave, the tattooed technician,
slips a pillow under my knees.

I want to tell him,
"My bones are shy.

I don't exercise.
I love coffee.

They know they're weak
and don't like being photographed."

Gust

Open the door
and wind

flaps its
dark wings,

turning umbrellas
inside out

like some higher-up
dropped

a cold stone
in a puddle of ink.

People blur,
        hurrying by,

but one white pigeon
circles
the bakery slowly,

unfazed,

eyeing a
rain-soaked baguette —

no room in her
bird brain

to curse
the weather.

If Next Week Is Good Friday

Today is Not Bad Friday —

sunny   soggy   milky

mild for March.

       Went to see *The Witch* (a movie)
       yesterday with Jerome.

       It is an accurate portrayal
       of how too much religion

       with too little distraction
       could be a recipe for disaster.

We stayed up late —

cookies   oranges   wine

and now I am transfixed,
staring into space.

Is staring a kind of prayer?

I think so — yes.

A bodiless male voice: "What's up?"
floats in a sound bubble past my window.

Another one answers: "There you go."

Today =

Brighter light
Lighter shadows

Cherry-blossom-Afros
on the trees

Ease
           of movement

in silky
butterscotch air

Coats open —

elbows and bare arms
appear

Finally, the body
untenses
           after winter

Birdsong
pours   la la la

between the words
and buildings

More Unisex Colognes

ALIBI

Buy two because you never know
when you'll need one.

Made from a complex blend
of masking fragrances,
this protean scent
will cover your tracks.

No questions asked.

MARTINI

Crisp. Dry. Pristine.

Perpetually chill.

Works equally well
in an office or casual setting.

Comes in three varieties:
olive, apple, lemon twist.

OBSCURITY

Soaking in this aromatic
elixir is like having your own
cloak of invisibility.

A centuries-old favorite of poets,
crackpots, and hermit monks.

Guaranteed to keep you
on the sidelines where
you'll get your best work done.

Perfume Dioramas

WE MARK OUR PLACE AND IT MARKS US

I enter the building — the room —
by a door, then another door.

But it enters me through the air
I breathe in

its commingling of human and animal,
mineral and chemical, cooking and debris.

A building is made in no small part
of air.

Yoko Ono tells us to bottle the air
at different hours,

and also to send smell signals
by wind.

Today is apples, smoke,
tentacles of vomit

left over on the sidewalk
as I fumble for my keys.

No shape
takes place
in time
without smell.

MY GRANDMOTHER'S GLASS SKYLINE

Shalimar
Emeraude
Tigress

gave her bungalow
in Chicago
an exotic air.

As a child,
looking up
at the geometry
of bottles
on her dresser,

I thought each
a liquid city —

and fragrance
the real magic carpet
to carry me there.

How wise the wizard
must have been
to shrink and imprison

a forest, an ocean,
a mountain —

a whole kingdom
in these glass towers.

PSYCHO-SCENTUAL

I once had a therapist
who practiced
olfactory analysis —

often declaring,
about any difficult situation,
person, or emotion I brought up:

"It stinks. It really stinks.
That just stinks all over the place."

He had a small windowless office
where oddly (I thought)
he continually burned
a vanilla-scented candle,

perhaps to infuse a more pleasing
mental attitude in his clients,
or as a form of self-protection
from the noxious cloud
of their negative energy.

It was a big deal for me
(never good at setting boundaries)
to ask him to please refrain
from keeping it lit during our sessions
as it aggravated my allergies.

He gladly complied,
but the smell of burnt sugar,
like an alter ego,

always lingered, and often
I found myself clearing my throat
as I struggled to find
the right words — and air —
to describe my experience.

THE BASEMENT LAUNDRY ROOM SMELLS

Like a combination of damp and dry things:

dirty socks, disinfectant, drains,
dust blown about by fans,

air freshener, fabric softener,

the cardboard smell of boxes
stacked up, each harboring the ghost smell
of what it used to contain,

the newspaper smell,

the broken smell of old furniture,
abandoned and soon to be carted off.

LIKE FORM, FRAGRANCE FOLLOWS FUNCTION

Not always literally —

banks don't really smell
of money.

Of credit, perhaps,
a deferral of smell
borrowed against the future.

And doesn't one find
in government buildings
the muffled odor of bureaucracy?

Scent is invisible architecture,

a binding together of place
with diffuse beams.

I cannot think of
Gothic cathedrals
as other than ornate
incense burners.

Cityscape

A choir of angles,
a chorus of sharps

scaling the jagged
perpendiculars.

Pedagogy

I can teach enthusiasm.

Discrimination is harder.

Hardest of all are the intangibles.

River of Students

Everything in my life seems vague and elusive, yet for the most part,
my sense of impermanence has turned out to be rather solid.

How else is it possible that for almost forty years I've been teaching —
sitting in any number of nondescript rooms, in front of blackboards
I never write on, exchanging pleasantries with the students as if we were
simply passing time by talking about books we happen to be reading.

I think of all their names, the papers they've handed me, the papers
I've handed back, and together we form a current — a kind of river
that has drawn me — drawn us — forward toward I'm not sure what.

Perhaps the larger ocean of language itself.

Chamomile Tea

Tired as always
of the harangue

's boomerang

whistling past an ear,

slicing the air
packed with pathological
allergens.

I'm sorry but
my sturm and drang
are dragging.

Today I wish for
nothing more,

if peace be out of reach,
than gentleness.

C-notes

for Ray DiPalma

corners
and coroners

civics
and cynics

calendars
and colanders

caliphs
and calipers

cupids
and cul-de-sacs

culprits
and calliopes

carnivals
and carnivores

chorales
and corollaries

Looking Out the Window in a Novel

1.

I don't even know my name.

I may not have one.

But I am here
and I am there,

an American poet
living in a French novel

where the rain, the traffic,
even the wind slurs and shushes

in that distinctive way I find so difficult
to mimic or comprehend,
yet it soothes me.

I told Anca, the author,
to look in the windows
of brownstones in New York.

I've always loved to study
the way objects are so dramatically
arranged and displayed in them.

How in one, a parrot perches on a globe;
in another, the curve of a piano gleams darkly.

Once an art dealer walking with me
recognized the blood-red corner of a painting
he'd sold peeking above the shade.

Anca said: "Thank you for the windows!
They will definitely find their way into my book,
and you'll be behind one of them
looking for a poem to emerge."

Then she went back to Paris.

2.

To be honest, I don't spend much time (like none)
looking out of my own window.

What I lack is a view, a vista, and all it implies —
looking down on a bus stop, lonesome at 3 a.m.,
a trio of headless mannequins waiting casually
in the window of the dress shop across the street.

I think I prefer to look into rather than out of.
Perhaps that's why I read novels.

I've never written a novel, but if I did I'm sure
it would begin with a woman looking out of a window
back at me.

3.

The unknown
world:
                    a passerby.

The windows:
                    a glass slide show
                    for studying culture.

O open or closed —
why do I keep returning?

I see you, windows,
as my protagonist.

4.

Dear Anca,

It was fun to meet you and live briefly
in your novel. I can't wait to read it

to find out what else (if anything)
happens to me — and everyone.

Here is the poem my character wrote.
It's called "Anon," as in anonymous,

but also as in I hope I see you again soon.

∎ ∎ ∎

The nights —

long blue dashes —

gulp the distance
between our days.

Windows
stacked
like pancakes

buttered
with light.

I walk in
what was,

is almost
still,

turning the corner
like a page,

the page
like a corner.

We have many times
met without meeting
like this,

at some dog-eared
intersection,

each in search of
the right words
for *color* or *tremor;*
stranger or *friend.*

Prolonging

I only had five pages to go until the end of the story, but it was taking forever to finish. Not because it wasn't interesting but because I began to suspect more words, new sentences, whole paragraphs previously not there were surreptitiously inserting themselves right under my nose. I couldn't prove it, but I became so convinced of the presence of this textual gremlin that I kept rereading certain passages hoping to catch it in the act while, at the same time, forgetting what was originally said, thus defeating my own purpose and, in the process, prolonging the final scene even further until it began to feel like one of those shots in a movie where a character keeps walking and walking and walking down a corridor for a very long time without getting any closer to the door. It was light when I first began to read, and now it's dark. I'm supposed to meet someone for dinner and already I'm running late, but there are only a few more pages, and I just have to know what happens.

Ash, Ether

Stubble of night.

The great chain
of being unchained —

the double helix
unstrung —

scattering beads,
beans,

language memes.

The sprawl of cities.

The scrawl of graffiti
clamoring over
high walls.

Jack who stole
the giant's
golden harp

was also David
who played it
for King Saul.

Retail Space for Rent

Every day emptiness erases

big franchises
as well as small boutiques:

the place that sold gadgets,
the shop that specialized in hats.

It's a commercial version
of the Rapture — leaving behind

a jigsaw puzzle of blank pieces,
each one an unopened invitation

to anyone with an ounce of creative vision
and the millions needed to back it up.

If this were a movie, aliens would be arriving
to set up their ministry,

but today even the sky seems vacant.

We're dissolving the past
faster than we can manufacture the future.

Lots of everything must go.
Not enough coming soon.

The World Being Unspoken

Listening backward —

dissolving the word
and its descendants

into a soft, amphibious
carpet of sound.

Hiss of stars
and gassy planets —

the rabbit
of the alphabet

drops back
into the void
of the black hat.

The Dead Rock Star

Is still insatiable.

His charisma travels
light-years —

a ghost in a strap-on body

continuously
pouring itself
over a writhing
audience.

I mean market.
I mean planet.

Vegging Out

Whitman
Lorca
Popeye

Hermes Trismegistus
L. Frank Baum

Teach me your green-
blooded anthems.

Find me a job
in an oxygen factory

converting
planks of light.

Green Tara's
mantra is circulating.

The Green Man is lost in the valley
of the Jolly Green Giant.

The Green Lantern is hanging out
along Green Dolphin Street.

The Green Lion sleeps
on the uncut hair of graves.

Notes

"Smile / Simile" was written for a collaborative project featuring eleven aquatints of smiling women by the artist Alex Katz, paired with poems by eleven writers. The poem appeared in the book *You Smile and the Angels Sing* (Lococo Fine Art Publisher, 2016).

"Mystery Poem" was written for *Conjunctions,* issue 63, *Speaking Volumes.*

"Jerome in Ten" and "Larry Eigner: In His Own Words" were inspired by Jonathan Williams's "Acrosticals." All of the words in the Larry Eigner piece are lines or parts of lines from his poems.

"A Part Of / Apart From" was written for a catalog accompanying an exhibit of nature photographs by Vivien Bittencourt at Ille Arts. The images were taken during her residency on Captiva Island, off the coast of Florida.

"Exquisite Corpse Pose" was compiled from notes in a journal I kept during a mindfulness meditation class.

"Perfume Dioramas" was written for *Conjunctions,* issue 68, *Inside Out: Architectures of Experience.*

LITERATURE
is not the same thing as
PUBLISHING

Coffee House Press began as a small letterpress operation in 1972 and has grown into an internationally renowned nonprofit publisher of literary fiction, essay, poetry, and other work that doesn't fit neatly into genre categories.

Coffee House is both a publisher and an arts organization. Through our *Books in Action* program and publications, we've become interdisciplinary collaborators and incubators for new work and audience experiences. Our vision for the future is one where a publisher is a catalyst and connector.

Funder Acknowledgments

Coffee House Press is an internationally renowned independent book publisher and arts nonprofit based in Minneapolis, MN; through its literary publications and *Books in Action* program, Coffee House acts as a catalyst and connector—between authors and readers, ideas and resources, creativity and community, inspiration and action.

Coffee House Press books are made possible through the generous support of grants and donations from corporations, state and federal grant programs, family foundations, and the many individuals who believe in the transformational power of literature. This activity is made possible by the voters of Minnesota through a Minnesota State Arts Board Operating Support grant, thanks to the legislative appropriation from the Arts and Cultural Heritage Fund. Coffee House also receives major operating support from the Amazon Literary Partnership, Jerome Foundation, McKnight Foundation, Target Foundation, and the National Endowment for the Arts (NEA). To find out more about how NEA grants impact individuals and communities, visit www.arts.gov.

Coffee House Press receives additional support from the Elmer L. & Eleanor J. Andersen Foundation; the David & Mary Anderson Family Foundation; Bookmobile; Dorsey & Whitney LLP; Foundation Technologies; Fredrikson & Byron, P.A.; the Fringe Foundation; Kenneth Koch Literary Estate; the Matching Grant Program Fund of the Minneapolis Foundation; Mr. Pancks' Fund in memory of Graham Kimpton; the Schwab Charitable Fund; Schwegman, Lundberg & Woessner, P.A.; the Silicon Valley Community Foundation; and the U.S. Bank Foundation.

The Publisher's Circle of Coffee House Press

Publisher's Circle members make significant contributions to Coffee House Press's annual giving campaign. Understanding that a strong financial base is necessary for the press to meet the challenges and opportunities that arise each year, this group plays a crucial part in the success of Coffee House's mission.

Recent Publisher's Circle members include many anonymous donors, Suzanne Allen, Patricia A. Beithon, the E. Thomas Binger & Rebecca Rand Fund of the Minneapolis Foundation, Andrew Brantingham, Robert & Gail Buuck, Dave & Kelli Cloutier, Louise Copeland, Jane Dalrymple-Hollo & Stephen Parlato, Mary Ebert & Paul Stembler, Kaywin Feldman & Jim Lutz, Chris Fischbach & Katie Dublinski, Sally French, Jocelyn Hale & Glenn Miller, the Rehael Fund-Roger Hale/Nor Hall of the Minneapolis Foundation, Randy Hartten & Ron Lotz, Dylan Hicks & Nina Hale, William Hardacker, Randall Heath, Jeffrey Hom, Carl & Heidi Horsch, the Amy L. Hubbard & Geoffrey J. Kehoe Fund, Kenneth & Susan Kahn, Stephen & Isabel Keating, Julia Klein, the Kenneth Koch Literary Estate, Cinda Kornblum, Jennifer Kwon Dobbs & Stefan Liess, the Lambert Family Foundation, the Lenfestey Family Foundation, Joy Linsday Crow, Sarah Lutman & Rob Rudolph, the Carol & Aaron Mack Charitable Fund of the Minneapolis Foundation, George & Olga Mack, Joshua Mack & Ron Warren, Gillian McCain, Malcolm S. McDermid & Katie Windle, Mary & Malcolm McDermid, Sjur Midness & Briar Andresen, Maureen Millea Smith & Daniel Smith, Peter Nelson & Jennifer Swenson, Enrique & Jennifer Olivarez, Alan Polsky, Marc Porter & James Hennessy, Robin Preble, Alexis Scott, Ruth Stricker Dayton, Jeffrey Sugerman & Sarah Schultz, Nan G. & Stephen C. Swid, Kenneth Thorp in memory of Allan Kornblum & Rochelle Ratner, Patricia Tilton, Joanne Von Blon, Stu Wilson & Melissa Barker, Warren D. Woessner & Iris C. Freeman, and Margaret Wurtele.

For more information about the Publisher's Circle and other ways to support Coffee House Press books, authors, and activities, please visit www.coffeehousepress.org/pages/support or contact us at info@coffeehousepress.org.

Elaine Equi's witty, aphoristic, and innovative work has become nationally and internationally known. Her book *Ripple Effect: New and Selected Poems* was a finalist for the L.A. Times Book Prize and shortlisted for the Griffin Poetry Prize. Among her other titles are *Sentences and Rain; Surface Tension; Decoy; Voice-Over,* which won the San Francisco State University Poetry Prize; and *The Cloud of Knowable Things.* She teaches at New York University and in the MFA program at the New School.

The Intangibles was designed by
Bookmobile Design & Digital Publisher Services.
Text is set in Minion Pro.